Magic Toys, Tricks and Illusions

It's fun to make your own tricks and toys, and there are lots to choose from in this book. All are made out of simple materials, and step-by-step instructions are given with plenty of clear diagrams. In no time at all you'll be able to baffle your friends with examples of mind-reading, amuse them with a writhing snake or a pair of swivelling eyes, and amaze them with an erupting volcano or a water drop microscope!

Eric Kenneway has written a number of books on crafts and origami. He is the author of *Paper Shapes*, *Paper Fun* and *Fingers, Knuckles and Thumbs*, all published by Beaver.

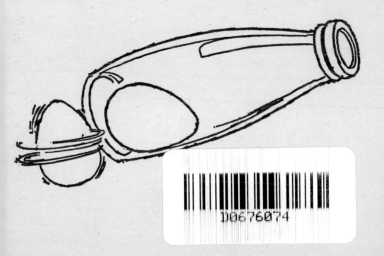

MAGIC
TOYS, TRICKS
AND ILLUSIONS

Eric Kenneway

Illustrated by Mike Jackson

Beaver Books

A Beaver Original
Published by Arrow Books Limited
62-65 Chandos Place, London WC2N 4NW

An imprint of Century Hutchinson Limited

London Melbourne Sydney Auckland
Johannesburg and agencies throughout
the world

First published in 1979
Seventh impression 1986

Set in Monotype Imprint

Printed and bound in Great Britain by
Anchor Brendon Limited, Tiptree, Essex

ISBN 0 09 939760 9

Contents

Magic toys that take longer to make

Foreword

Everybody likes surprises – if they are nice ones – and there are plenty of good ones here. In the following pages you will find tricks and illusions which will surprise not only your friends but you too, even while you are performing them.

Those of you who enjoy making things can also find out how to make toys to provide longer-lasting enjoyment. You may even see something which you think suitable to make as a present for a grown-up.

Each project starts with a list of the things you need. Decorate the toys in your own way, with paints or inks or coloured paper, and try to think of ways in which a toy may be adapted to make something quite new.

Most important, remember that cutting instruments, especially craft knives, can be very sharp. If you are using a craft knife, do your cutting-out on a piece of old board so that you don't injure yourself or scratch any surfaces. Always keep your tools in a safe place, preferably a box with a lid, and make sure that they are out of the reach of small brothers and sisters.

I am indebted to those two great Victorian popularisers of parlour magic, 'Tom Tit' and 'Professor Hoffman', who originated or first recorded some of the ideas in this book; and I also wish to thank John French for his help.

E.K.

SIMPLE TRICKS
AND ILLUSIONS

Spinning coin

You will need: 10p piece (or other milled edge coin)
two dressmaker's pins

Lay your coin on the table and pick it up between the
points of two pins. Blow gently on the coin and it will
spin around.

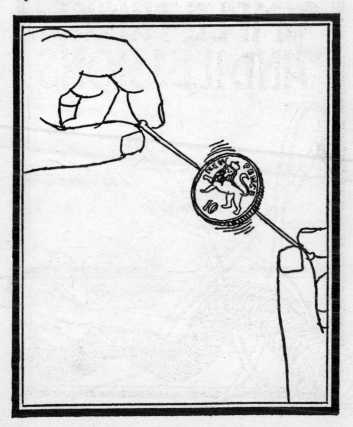

Standing egg

You will need: hard boiled egg
                        tray

1 Place a hard boiled egg on a tray and start the egg spinning with a vigorous turn of your wrist.

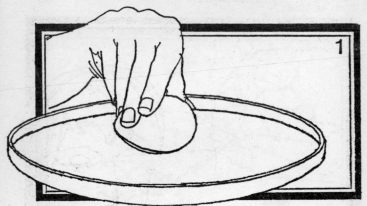

2 The egg will raise itself, as it spins, until it is balancing on one end.

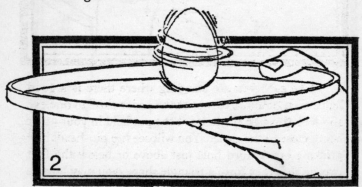

Double vision

You will need: pin
paper

1 Prick out two holes, about 1.5 mm apart, in one corner of a sheet of paper.

2 Make sure you are standing where there is a good light, then hold the corner of the paper close to one eye and look through the holes at the pin held in your other hand, close to the paper. You will see *two* pin-heads! By pricking out a third hole just above or below the first two, so that they form a triangle shape, you may be able to see *three* pinheads when you look through the holes.

Long or short?

You will need: pencil
ruler
paper

1 Draw two straight, parallel lines. Make sure they are both exactly the same length – say, 5 cm long and about 2 cm apart.

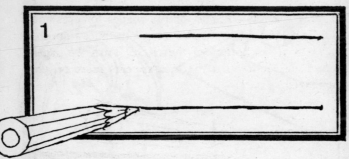

2 Then draw angles like this at the ends of the lines. You *know* the parallel lines are both the same length because you drew them, but perhaps your friends will find it difficult to believe that one is not shorter than the other.

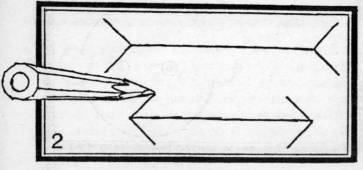

Two-way faces

You will need: pencil
paper

Have you ever tried drawing two faces in one? It can be fun to draw a face, then turn it around and find a quite different face which you did not realise you had drawn at all! Here is a way to get started on two-way faces:

1 Draw a circle and add simple shapes for eyes and ears. These should be about the same distance from the top as from the bottom of the circle. Turn the paper around and notice that the face appears more or less unchanged.

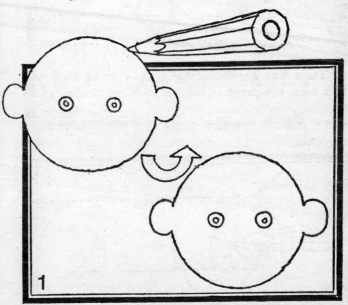

2 Draw a simple shape to represent a nose. This, too, should lie in the centre of the circle. Turn it around and the face is till more or less the same.

3 Now try adding a moustache. When turned around it becomes a pair of eyebrows.

4 A line for the mouth becomes a wrinkle in the forehead.

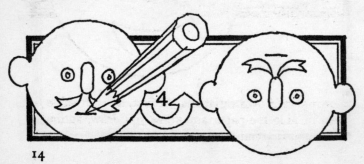

5 A lock of hair becomes a smiling mouth.

Now try your own variations. At first, it is advisable to keep turning the paper around as you draw, adding a bit to one face and then a bit to the other.

Magic rings

You will need: strip of paper, about 4 cm x 30 cm
or longer
glue
scissors

1 Make one complete twist in the paper strip . . .

2 . . . and glue the two ends together.

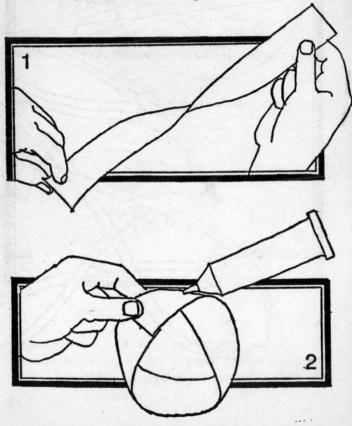

3 Now cut around the centre of the ring.

4 The result is not two rings, as you might have supposed, but one big ring.

Cut all the way around the centre as before. This will make an even bigger ring, won't it?

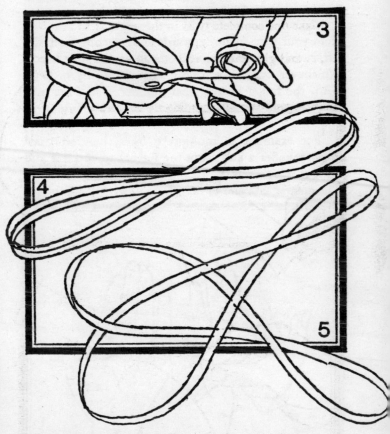

5 Wrong. This time you have made two rings.

Mysterious number nine

You will need: pair of hands

There is something mysterious about the number 9. For one thing it is possible to multiply any number by 9 very quickly on your fingers.

Hold your hands palm upwards and, starting from the left, number your fingers from 1 to 10 (in your head). Whichever number you wish to multiply by 9, bend down the finger bearing that number. Then see how many fingers are left standing up on either side of it.

1   For example, to multiply 9 by 2, bend forward finger number 2 and count the fingers to the left and right of it.
The answer is 1 and 8, i.e. 18.

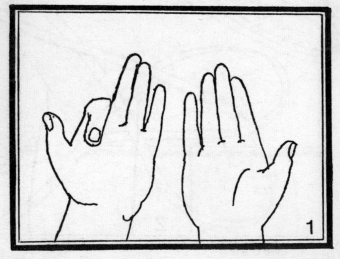

2 To multiply 9 by 3, bend down finger number 3 and you will see that the answer is 2 and 7, i.e. 27.

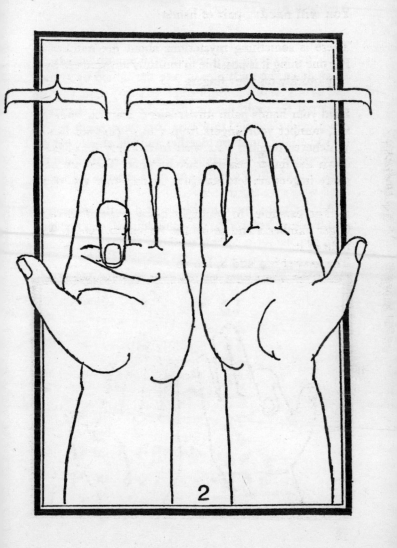

2

From nine to nine

You will need: pencil

paper

Write down the figure 9 and, in a column underneath it, write down the multiples of 9 (9 multiplied by 2, by 3 and so on) up to 9 multiplied by 10 (if you like, you can work out the multiples by using the method shown on the previous page). Draw two lines underneath.

Add all the numbers together and you should get the answer 495. Add each digit, 4, 9 and 5, together and the answer is 18. Add 1 and 8 and the answer is 9 – we are back where we started.

Add as many more multiples of 9 to the column as you like – 99, 108 and so on – and you will still finish up with the answer 9 by this method.

$$
\begin{array}{r}
9 \\
18 \\
27 \\
36 \\
45 \\
54 \\
63 \\
72 \\
81 \\
+\ 90 \\
\hline
495 \\
\hline
\end{array}
$$

$$4 + 9 + 5 = 18$$
$$1 + 8 = 9$$

Mind-reading

You will need: pencil
paper

Here is a little 'mind-reading act' to try on a friend. Tell him to write down a three-digit number – any number he likes provided the digits decrease in value (e.g. 6, 4 and 3), and not to let you see what he has written. Then tell him to write the same number backwards underneath (e.g. 3, 4 and 6). Now tell him to take one number away from the other. When he has worked out the answer, ask him what the final digit is (7 in our example). You will immediately be able to tell him that the remaining hidden digits are 2 and 9.

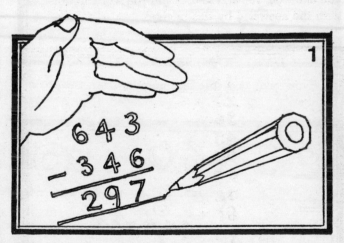

How you do it: once you know the final digit, take it away from 9 to find the first digit; and the middle digit is 9 always, no matter what numbers you start with.

More mind-reading

You will need: pencil
paper

Make sure your friend has a pencil and paper and tell him to write down any number he likes provided the digits do not decrease in value. Tell him to keep the number hidden from you; then instruct him as follows:

1 'Multiply the number you wrote down by 10.'

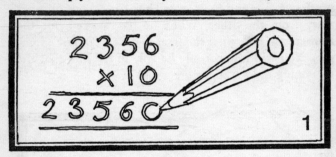

2 'Now take away the first number from the second number.'

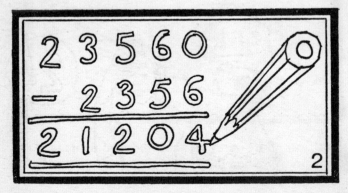

3 'Add 9 to the answer.'

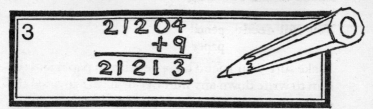

4 'Cross out any one digit you like except for a nought and tell me what the remaining digits are.'

5 Add these remaining digits together in your head and take the total from 9 to find what digit was crossed out. In our example, the remaining digits total 7. After taking this away from 9 you can tell your friend that you know it was a 2 he crossed out.

They went whataway?

You will need: small sheet of paper
pencil
tumbler
jug of water

1 Fold the sheet of paper in half and draw an arrow in the middle of one side.

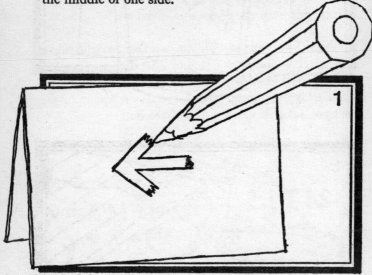

2 Stand the paper on the table and place an empty, straight-sided tumbler a little way in front of it. Challenge your friends to turn the arrow around without touching the paper or the glass.

3 You do it by producing a jug of water and filling the tumbler with water. The arrow will immediately turn and face the opposite way!

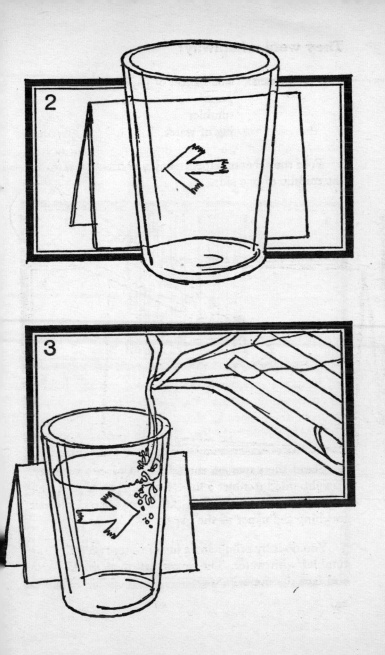

Long letters

You will need: pencil
paper

1 You can write messages which should be difficult to read for anybody who is not in the know – not necessarily by using a code, but simply by lengthening the letters greatly.

2 Read the message by shutting one eye and holding the paper close to the other. The letters now appear to have their normal shape. Move the paper from right to left and let the letters pass in front of your eye.

Writhing snake

You will need: tissue paper, about 10 cm × 12 cm
                     pencil
                     water

1   Roll your rectangle of paper around a pencil.

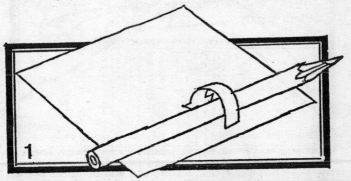

2   Push down one edge of the tissue paper with your thumbnail.

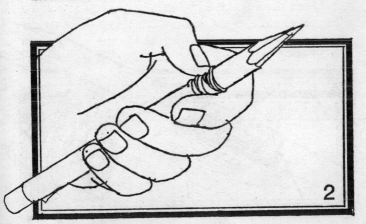

3 Squeeze the tissue paper carefully along the pencil from the other end . . .

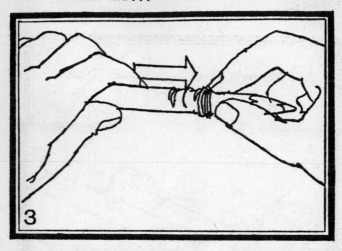

4 . . . until it is squeezed into the middle of the pencil like this. Slip it off the pencil.

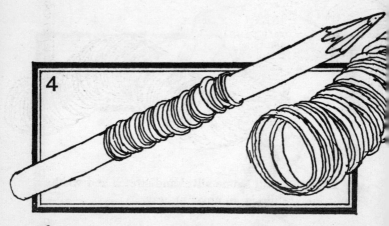

5 Place it on a suitable surface – the draining board of a sink perhaps – and allow one or two drops of water to fall on it.

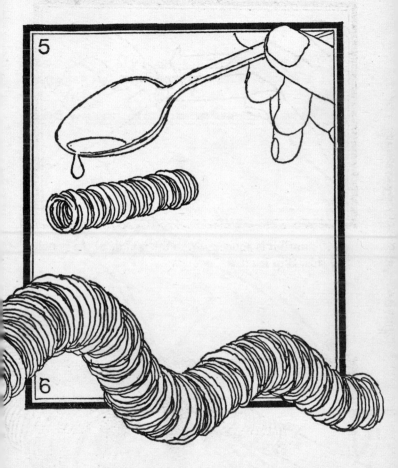

6 The snake will 'come alive' and stretch and writhe about for a while in an amazing way.

Egg in bottle

You will need: milk bottle
egg
cupful of vinegar

1 Find an egg just small enough to fit into the mouth of a milk bottle; slide it in carefully so that it does not break.

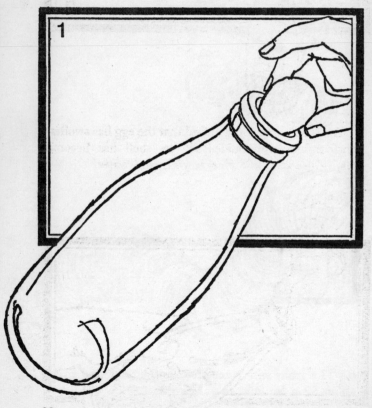

2 Pour about a cupful of vinegar into the bottle – just enough to cover the egg – and leave it for about twenty-four hours.

3 After this time you will find that the egg has swollen considerably (and incidentally its shell has become soft). Rinse away the vinegar with cold water.

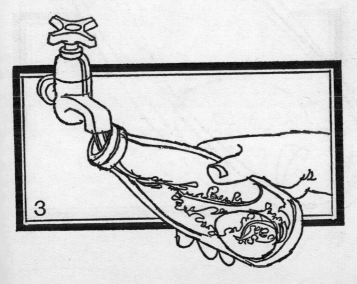

4 You now have an egg much too large to get out of the bottle. Display it and people will wonder how you ever got it in there!

By the way, you should throw the egg and bottle away after a couple of days, as the egg will start to smell a bit odd!

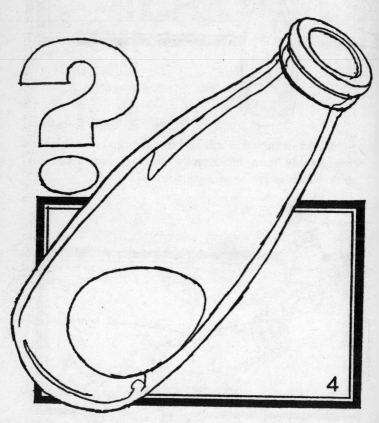

4

EASY-TO-MAKE MAGIC TOYS

Magic octagon

You will need: paper
pencil
ruler
scissors

1 Fold a sheet of paper in half . . .

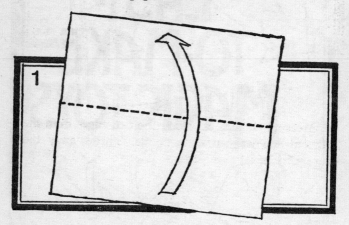

2 . . . then fold it in half the other way.

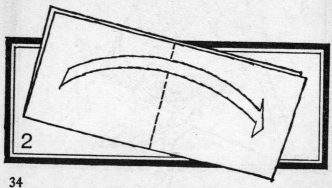

3 Bring the two folded edges together.

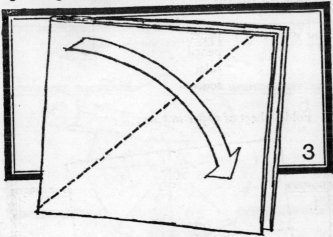

4 Measure about 4 cm along the two edges from the left and cut between these points. Throw away the large piece of leftover paper.

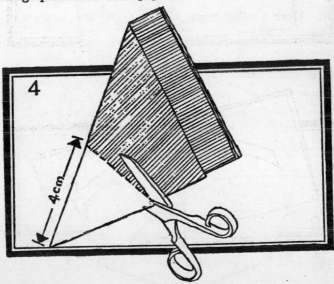

5 Open up the paper and flatten out the creases. Draw a large arrow at the top left as shown.

Turn the paper over. (*Note*: it is most important that you turn it over in the direction shown.)

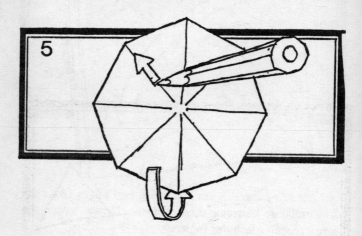

6 Draw another arrow, similar to the first, at the top left.

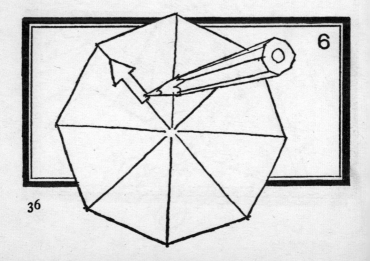

7 The magic octagon is complete and ready for use.
What you do with it: hold it so that the arrow is at the top left. Point to the arrow so that your friends remember its position.

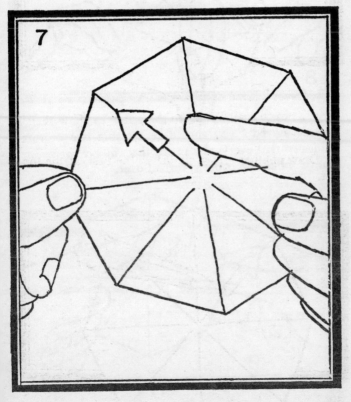

8 Quickly flip the octagon in the direction shown and . . .

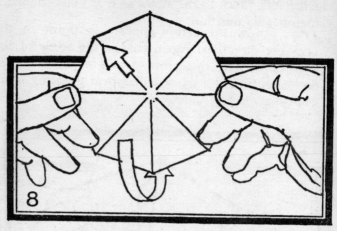

9 . . . once again, point to the arrow to show that 'it hasn't moved'. You should repeat this two or three times so that everyone can see that the arrow 'doesn't move' when the paper is turned over.

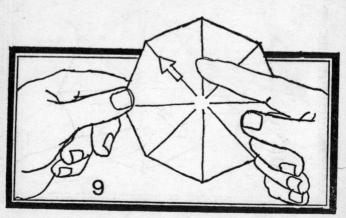

10 Then change the angle at which you are holding the octagon so that the arrow points to top right. Turn the paper over and ...

11 ... now the arrow appears to point in the opposite direction! Again change the angle of the octagon to point the arrow various ways; turn over and each time the arrow will appear pointing in an unexpected direction.

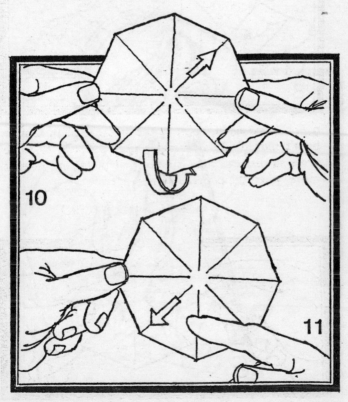

Instant string animals

You will need: one piece of string about 50 cm long

1   Hold one end of the string between your teeth and twist the string in the same direction as its thread (you can see which way this goes if you look carefully at the string first).

2 When you have twisted the string as much as you can, pull it taut and put a finger halfway along its length. Bring the two ends of the string together . . .

3 . . . like this. Remove your finger from the bottom and . . .

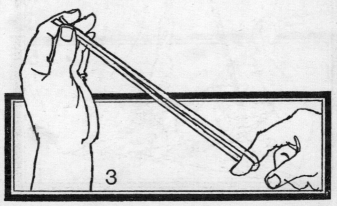

4 ... the two strands should immediately wind themselves together.

5 It can be fun to make animals from a piece of twisted string like this – not because the results are particularly splendid or even life-like, but because the animals somehow seem to make themselves!

Start by making a knot at the top to represent a head; the two ends will form ears.

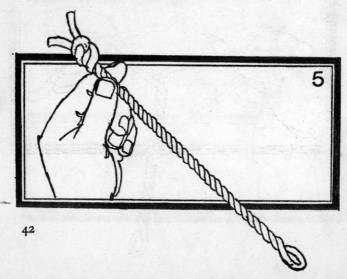

6 Put the string down on a flat surface and pull the two strands apart . . .

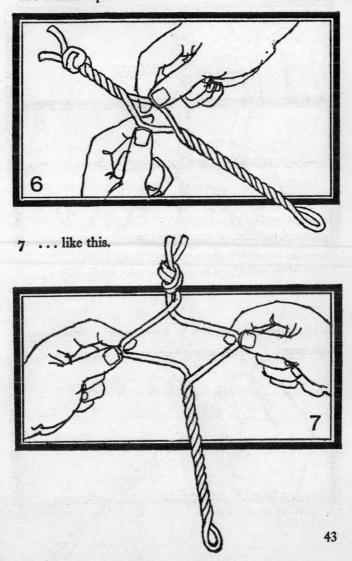

7 . . . like this.

8 Let go of the string and two legs will twist themselves into place. Pull the strings apart lower down . . .

9 . . . and two more legs will spring into place.

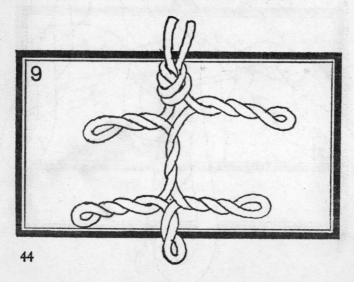

10 Stand your string animal up and with more string try making other kinds of creature.

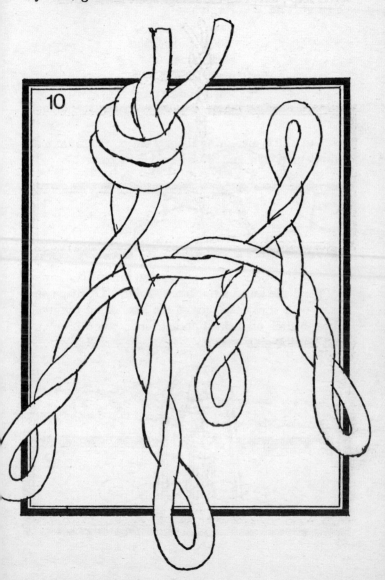

Water drop microscope

You will need: empty can
pin
old pair of scissors
sticky tape
glass
small pocket torch
drop of water

1 Cut a strip measuring about 2 cm × 10 cm from an empty metal can, and prick a hole in its centre.

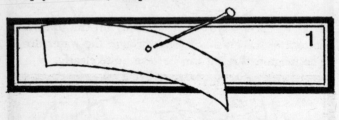

2 Bend the metal strip into a shallow 'U' shape and fix it with sticky tape across the base of an upturned glass. Switch on a small pocket torch, stand it on end and put the glass over it.

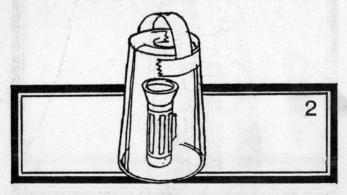

3 Let a drop of water fall on the pin hole; this forms a lens.

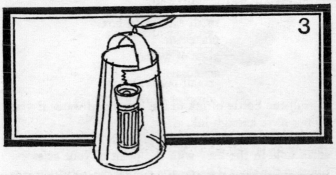

4 Put whatever you want to study on the upturned bottom of the glass and look through the water drop. The magnified result can be seen quite clearly.

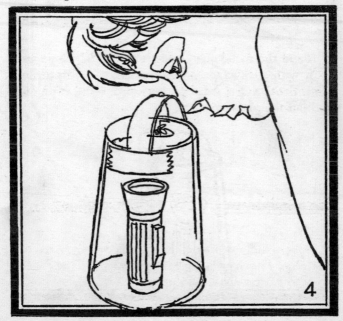

Volcano

You will need: bottle of ink
small cardboard box
plasticene
glass of water
scissors

1 Fill the bottle of ink to the brim; add water if you do not have enough ink.

Turn the cardboard box upside down and make a small hole in the base with the point of your scissors. Shorten the sides if necessary, so that the upturned box will rest on top of the ink bottle when placed over it.

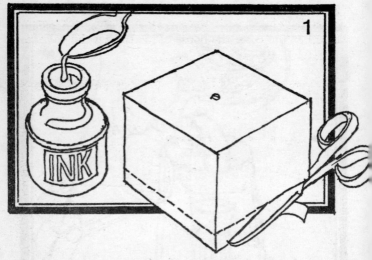

2 Make a hollow model of a little volcano out of plasticene, covering the hole in the box. Press the edges firmly to fix the volcano in place.

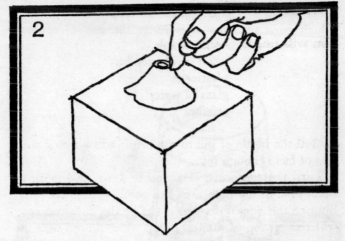

3 Pick up the box, with its volcano, and turn it over a glass half-filled with water. Turn these back again together and cover the bottle of ink so that the volcano is immediately above the ink.

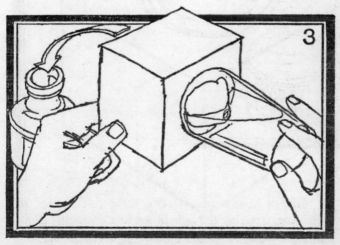

4 The volcano will appear to erupt. The 'smoke' which curls up from it is really the ink, of course, rising into the less dense water.

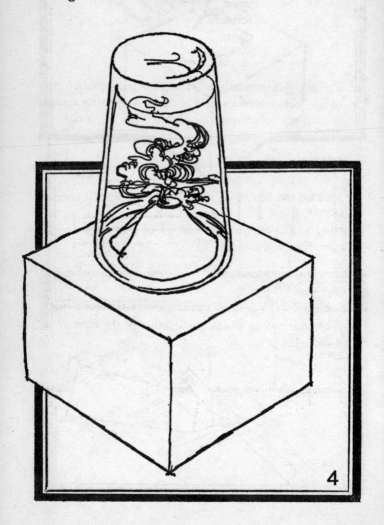

4

Magic folder

You will need: pencil
ruler
scissors
paper
thin card
glue

1 Prepare two rectangles of card measuring about 6 cm × 10 cm. Prepare two strips of paper measuring about 1 cm × 10 cm and two strips about 1 cm × 12 cm.

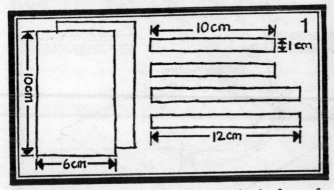

2 Glue the two 12 cm strips together in the form of a cross like this.

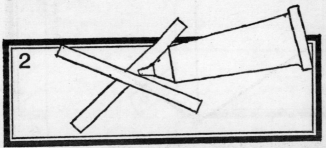

3 Place the cross centrally on one of the rectangular cards; bend the right-hand ends, marked B, back behind the card and turn it over.

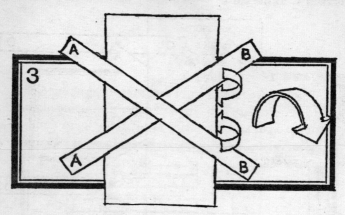

4 Glue the ends marked B to the card.

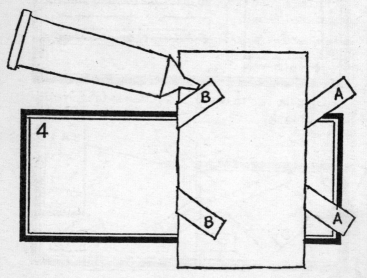

5 Place the 10 cm strips into position on the right, overlapping the card about 2 cm. Glue the two ends marked C to the card.

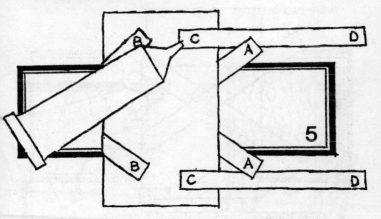

6 Slip the second card into place like this and glue the ends marked A to it.

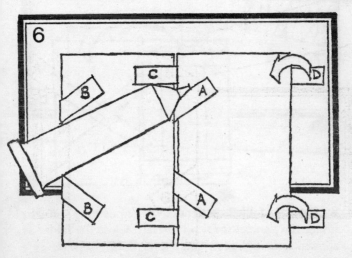

7 Fold over and glue the ends marked D to the card. This completes the magic folder's construction but you can improve its appearance by sticking fancy paper to these two surfaces.

Turn it over.

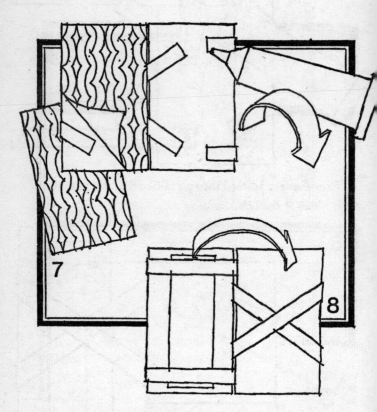

8 Place a folded banknote, or something similar, under the *parallel strips* on the left. Close the folder as shown, closing the left 'page' over the right page.

9 Now open it out *to the right* and . . .

10 . . . the note is under the *crossed strips* on the right!

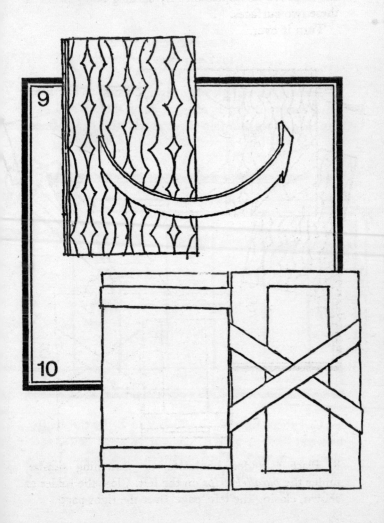

Swivel eyes

You will need: two pencils
ruler
paper
scissors or craft knife
inks or paints for decoration

1 Prepare a rectangle of paper measuring 10 cm × 18 cm. Measure intervals of 3 cm along the top and bottom long edges and join these points with pencil lines.

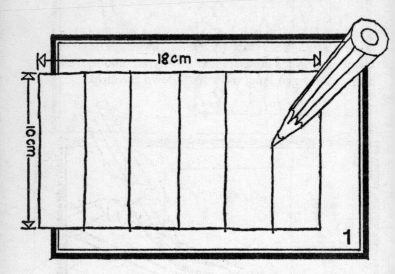

2 Call these lines A, B, C, D and E. In the centre, between lines A and B, cut out two eye holes, each about 1 cm wide. Then, between lines D and E, cut two horizontal slits above and below the level of the eye holes, about 3 cm apart.

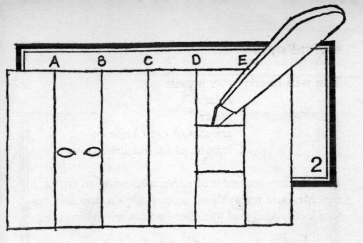

3 Prepare a strip of paper 3 cm wide and 20 cm or more in length. Hold two thick-tipped pencils or coloured crayons so that their points are about 1 cm apart. Draw two long, wavy lines down the strip.

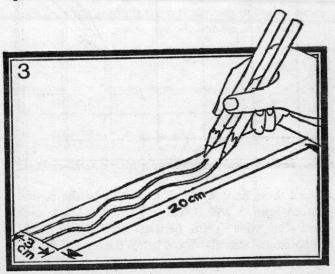

4 Turn the strip over and weave it through the two
slits cut in step 2.

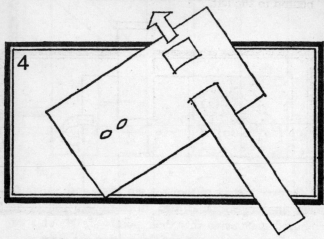

5 Fold forward the top and bottom edges of the strip.
(This is just to prevent it from slipping out.)
  Draw a face around the eye holes.

6 Fold the right-hand edge of the rectangle of paper behind to the left.

7 Move the strip up and down and the eyes will swivel suspiciously from side to side.

Snow scene

You will need: screw-top jar
plasticene
silver foil
scissors
paper
water

1 Clean the screw-top jar thoroughly; remove the label, if there is one, and make sure any dried glue is scrubbed off. Take off the lid and build a plasticene base for your scene inside it. Leave plenty of room around the edge of the lid and make sure you fix the plasticene firmly by pressing down and sealing any gaps at the sides.

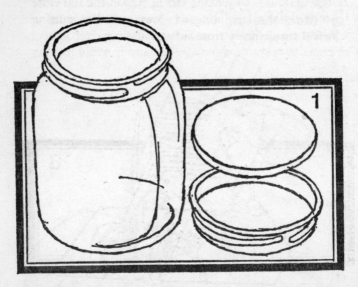

2 On the base, build a scene with more plasticene. Pick a subject which has something tall in it as a centre of interest – a church with a spire, a famous monument or a lighthouse will do.

3 Now cut the snow from a scrap of silver foil. It is easiest to do this by making lots of cuts in the foil close to each other all pointing one way and then cutting across these narrow strips. Do your cutting over a sheet of paper to keep the snow together and to avoid making a mess.

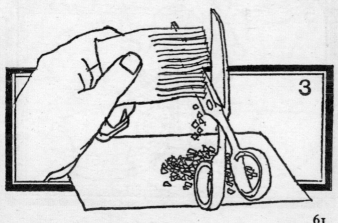

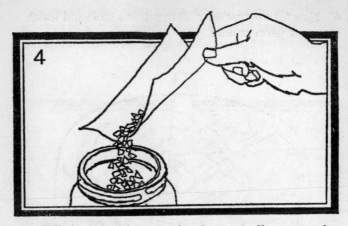

4 Fill the jar with water, leaving a small space at the top; then pour in the 'snow'.

5 Screw the lid back on to the jar tightly. (You had better do this over the sink in case some water is forced out.)

6 Now turn the jar over. Stand it on a table and watch the snow whirl around.

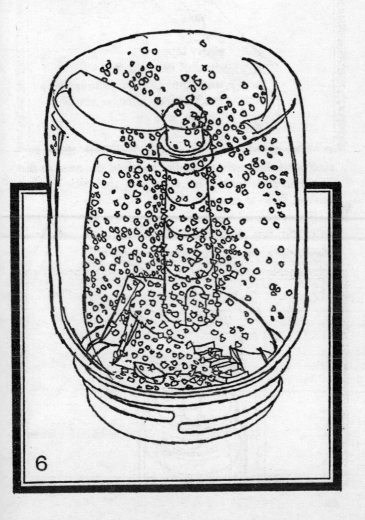

6

Simple kaleidoscope

You will need: pencil
                     ruler
                     scissors
                     glue
                     sticky tape
                     sheet of cellophane
                     thick card (e.g. mounting card)
                     two handbag mirrors, about
                         6 cm × 9 cm

1 Measure the two mirrors and prepare three rectangles of thick card of similar width to the mirrors but just a little longer. Glue a card to the back of each mirror, flush at one end.

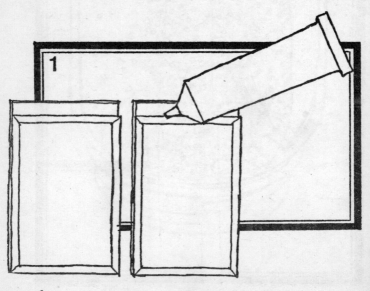

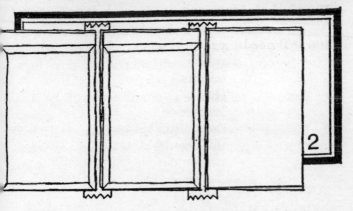

2 Join the long sides of the three cards together with sticky tape, leaving a gap between the cards. (It does not matter in which order they are arranged.)

3 Bring the two unattached sides together and join them with sticky tape in the same way. This will make a three-sided tube, with the mirrors facing inwards.

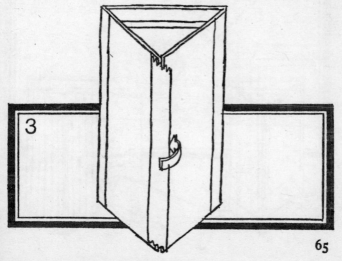

4 Place one end of the tube (the end with which the mirrors are flush) on to a sheet of cellophane. Cut the cellophane into a rough triangle a little larger than the tube, then cut away as shown and raise the three flaps.

5 Fasten the cellophane to the tube with sticky tape.

6 This completes the simple kaleidoscope, but it will look better if you decorate its sides with fancy paper.

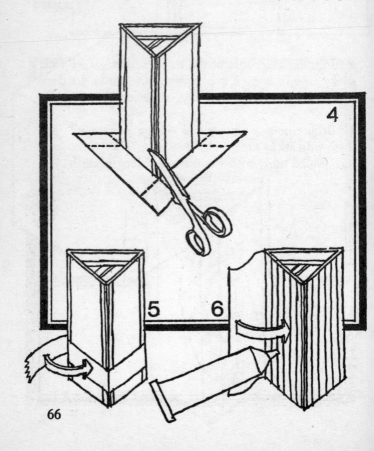

7 Hold the open end to one eye and place your fingertips along the edge of the other end. You will see a pattern something like the one shown here. Move your fingertips about to make an 'exploding flower' pattern.

Hold your kaleidoscope against a magazine page – one with coloured pictures. Face the light and move the magazine about. You will see all sorts of interesting patterns.

Walking policeman

You will need: pencil
ruler
thin card
scissors
pair of compasses
paper fastener
inks or paints to decorate

1 Prepare a rectangle of card about 7 cm × 12 cm.
Draw a policeman (or some other figure if you prefer),
without legs and facing sideways. Make sure he fills up
as much of the card as possible.

2 Cut around the figure and throw away the scraps.

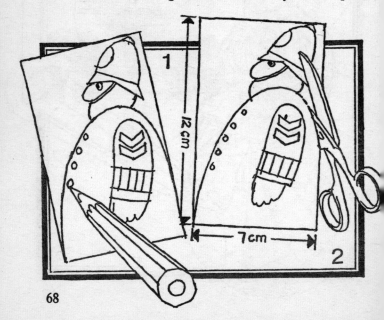

3 Now prepare a disc of card with a radius (the distance from the centre to the edge) of about 3 cm. Lightly draw the vertical and horizontal centre lines.

4 Draw more lines on either side of the centre lines, as shown.

5 You now have four trouser bottoms. Draw a boot on each one, facing the same way as the 'body' you have already made, and colour them in.

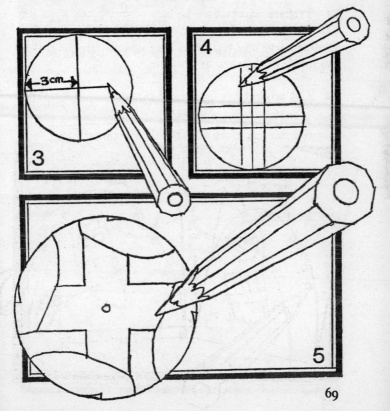

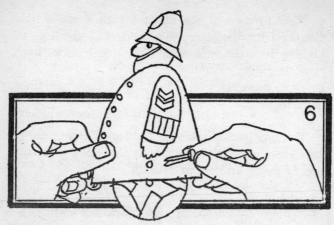

6 Attach the centre of the disc to the bottom end of the policeman's body with a paper fastener.

7 Now 'walk' your policeman across a table top and watch his legs go round. You will find that a cloth-covered table is more suitable than a smooth one.

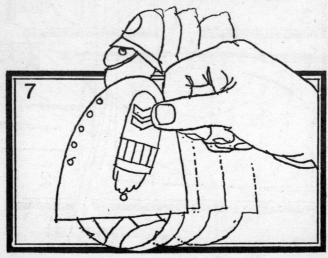

Jumping frogs

You will need: pencil
paper
scissors
empty box with cellophane window
in lid

1 Cut out a few little scraps of paper, about 4 or 5 cm square. Fold them in half.

2 With the fold at the left, draw this shape on to each piece and cut along the broken lines. Throw away the shaded areas.

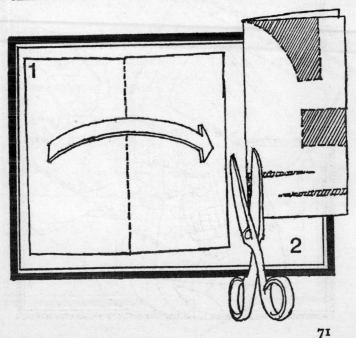

3 Fold at the joints to give form to your paper frogs.
Draw eyes.

4 Put the frogs in the box and close the lid.

5 Rub the outside of the cellophane window, and the frogs will jump up and down! This is because your rubbing creates static electricity.

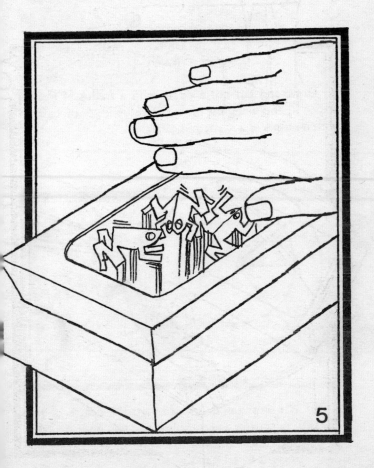

Water lily

You will need: paper
pencil
ruler
scissors
pair of compasses
45° set square
bowl of water

1 Draw and cut out a circle with a radius of 6 cm. Inside it, and using the same centre point, draw circles with a radius of 4.5 cm and 3 cm.

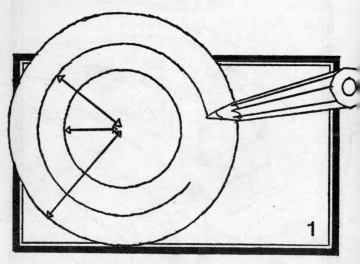

1

2 Draw a horizontal line through the centre of the disc. On this, draw a vertical line and two lines at 45° to it. Continue these lines in the lower half to divide the disc into eight equal parts.

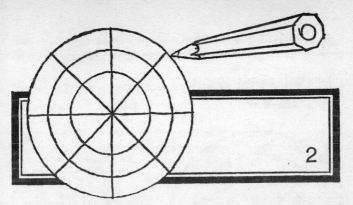

3 Mark the edge of the outer circle at points halfway between the radial lines.

4 Draw curved lines from these points to where the radial lines meet the second circle.

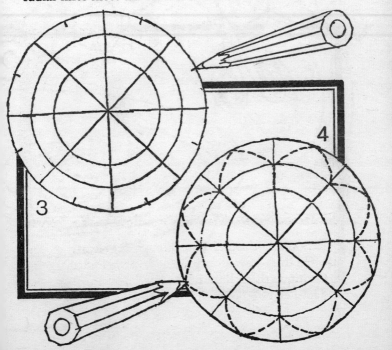

5 Now cut out the flower shape. To form petals, cut along the radial lines to the central circle, as shown.

6 Fold the tip of each 'petal' in turn to the centre point and make a firm crease so that they overlap ...

7 . . . and tuck one edge of the final petal under the first one folded.

8 Place your paper flower on the surface of a bowl of water and leave it. Very, very gradually the flower will open and spread its petals. It may be twenty minutes or half and hour before it opens fully, so why not spend the time making one or two more water lilies? A bowl full of flowers, all at various stages of opening, can look very attractive.

MAGIC TOYS THAT TAKE LONGER TO MAKE

Tumbling man

You will need: pencil
paper
scissors
glue
ruler
plasticene
inks or paints to decorate

1 Roll some plasticene between the palm of your hand and a flat surface to make a ball about 1.5 cm in diameter.

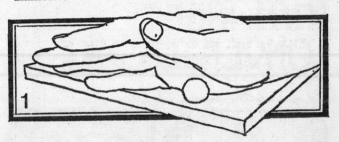

2 Prepare a rectangle of paper about 4 cm × 8 cm. Bend it into a tube, overlapping the two shorter edges by about 1 cm.

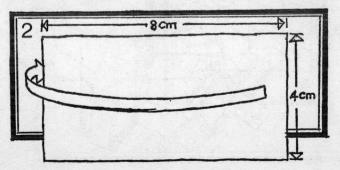

3 Glue the overlapping edges together.

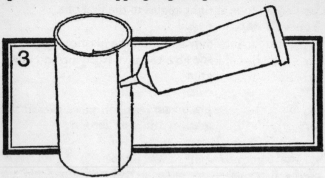

4 Prepare another sheet of paper 4 cm × 5 cm. Cut this into four 1 cm × 5 cm strips.

5 Make an arch out of one of these strips and glue it to one end of the tube. It should overlap the tube by about 1 cm on each side.

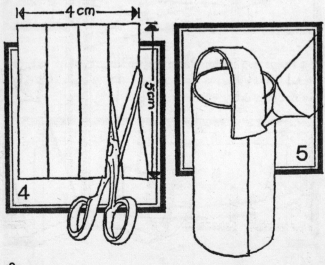

6 Now make another arch and glue this over the same end of the tube at right angles to the first one.

7 Turn the tube over and drop the plasticene ball into it. The ball should be able to move freely up and down inside the tube.

8 Glue the remaining two strips in place to seal the other end of the tube.

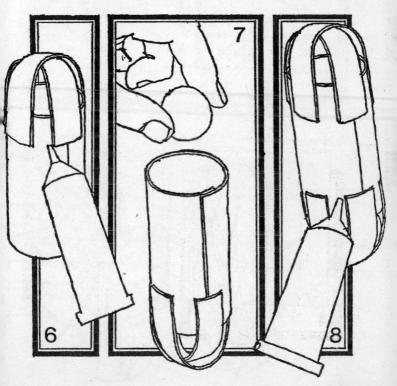

9 Draw a face on the tube.

10 From scraps of paper about 2 cm × 4 cm, cut out arms and legs.

11 Glue these to the body. Decorate with colours to complete the figure.

12 Put the tumbling man on a sloping surface (tilt a table if possible) and let go of him. He will somersault head-over-heels to the bottom of the slope.

Flicker book

You will need: pencil
ruler
thin card
scissors
pair of compasses
protractor
stapler
sticky tape

1 Prepare at least twelve cards, measuring about 3 cm × 8 cm. Stack these together and prick right through them with a pin (or the point of your compasses), towards the right-hand end.

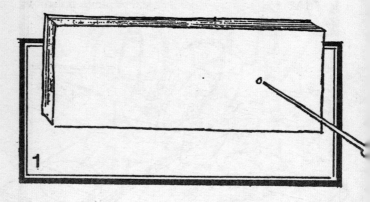

2 With the pin prick as centre, draw a circle on each card. Then draw a stripe across each circle. The angle of each stripe should be about fifteen degrees greater than the last one you drew.

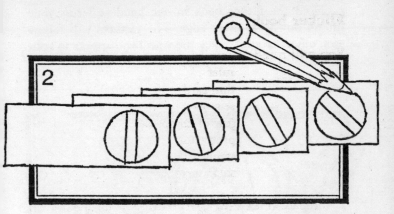

3 Stack the cards neatly in order and staple them together at the left.

4 Wrap some sticky tape over the staple to finish off.

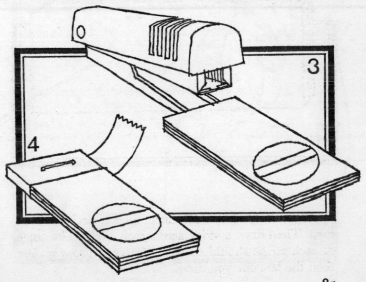

5 Hold the flicker book in one hand and run your thumb down the other edge. The pictures will follow each other so quickly that the wheel will appear to spin around as you watch it.

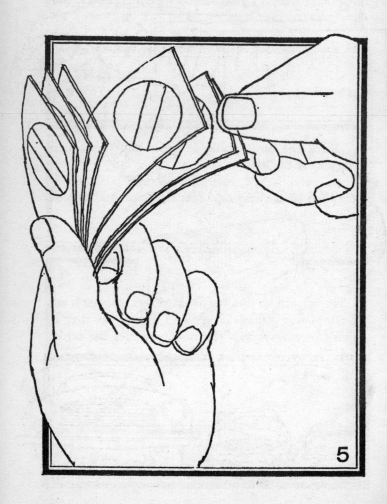

5

Ideas for flicker books

1 A circle divided into differently coloured sections, like a beach ball, is a good subject for a flicker book and quite easy to draw.

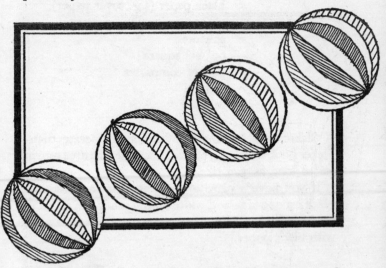

2 You might also try drawing an object, such as a car or aeroplane, getting bigger and bigger so that it appears to race towards you when you flick the cards.

Flicker wheel

You will need: pencil
ruler
thick card (e.g. mounting card)
black paper (e.g. cover paper)
glue
scissors
60° set square
pair of compasses
pin
mirror

A flicker wheel is more satisfying to operate than a flicker book because you can keep the pictures moving for as long as you like.

If you have a piece of card, at least 20 cm square, black on one side and white on the other, then you are ready to begin. If not, then cover one side of your card with black paper.

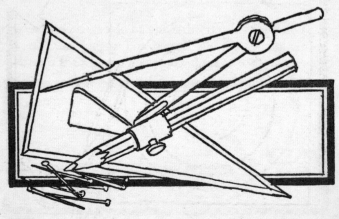

1 Draw a circle with a radius of 10 cm. Inside it, draw a circle of 7.5 cm radius and then one of 4 cm radius, using the same centre.

2 Cut around the outer circle to make a disc.

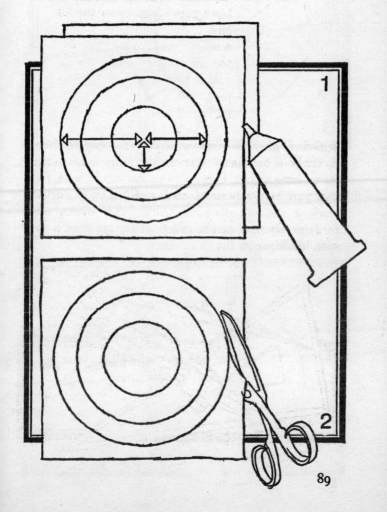

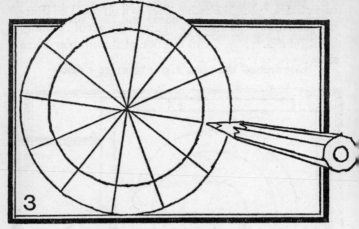

3 Draw a horizontal line through the centre, then draw a series of 30° angles from the centre with your set square to divide the disc into twelve equal parts.

4 From the rim to the outer circle, cut slits 8 mm wide, centered on the radial lines.

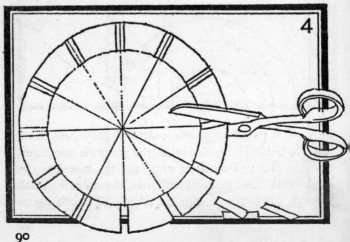

5 Now draw a series of twelve pictures between the two circles, using the radial lines as a guide. The illustration shows drawings of a figure in the act of running, but if you prefer you can use one of the simpler ideas shown on page 87.

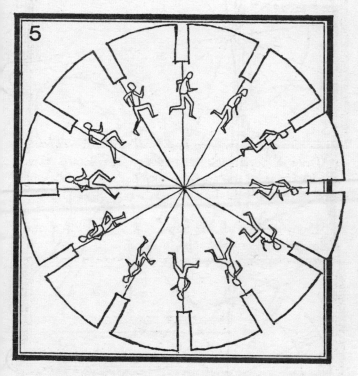

6 Push a pin through the centre of the wheel, from front to back. Hold the end of the pin with one hand; stand in front of a mirror and raise the wheel to eye level, with the pictures towards the mirror. Look through the slits and spin the wheel. The little figure will start to run at great speed. As the wheel slows he will seem to tire, but spin the wheel again and he will quicken his pace.

Having made one flicker wheel of card, you may like to try drawing pictures of other actions on paper discs of 7.5 cm radius. These can be slipped over the wheel you have already made and lightly attached to it to give you a variety of shows.

Magic colour-creating whizzer

You will need: thick white card (e.g. mounting
card)
scissors or craft knife
pencil
ruler
45° set square
pair of compasses
black paper
glue
thin string (at least 1 metre long)
neon light

You can make a simple whizzer of your own design and
not use the patterns shown here. But if you do take the
trouble to follow these unpromising-looking patterns
you will have the unexpected pleasure of turning black
and white into whirling reds and greens.

1   Prepare a disc of white card of 6 cm radius. Draw on
it circles of 4 cm and 2 cm radius, one inside the other,
using the same centre for both.

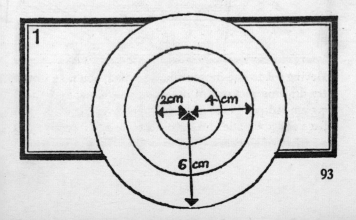

2 Draw horizontal and vertical lines through the centre; then draw lines through the centre at 45°, to divide the disc into eight sections.

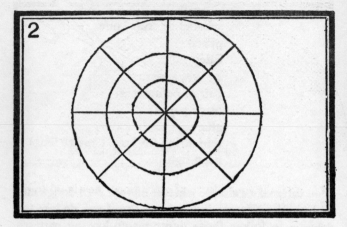

3 Prepare a half-circle of black paper of 6 cm radius. Draw radial lines and half-circles similar to the lines on the disc of card.

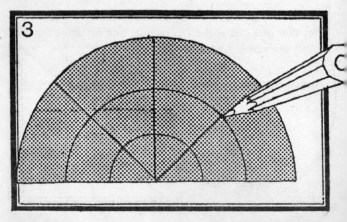

4 Cut along the dotted lines as shown to divide the black paper into four irregular shapes.

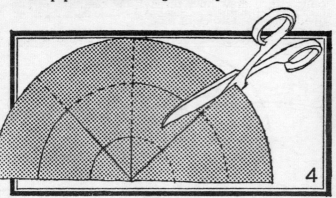

5 Stick the four pieces of black paper neatly on to the disc as shown.

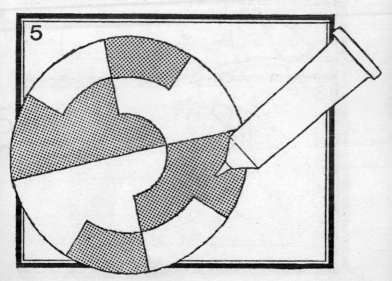

6 Make two holes in the centre of the disc, about 1 cm apart. Use the point of your scissors to do this. Thread the string through these holes and tie the ends together to form a loop.

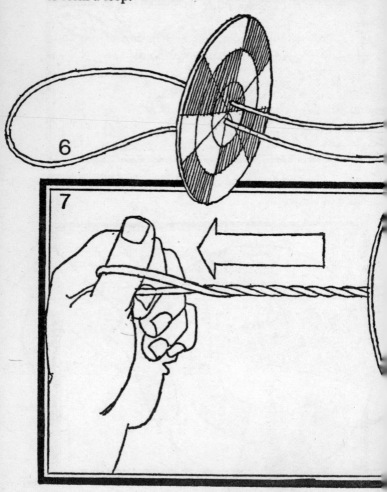

7 Hold the ends of the loop with your thumbs. Start twisting the string by making a few circular motions with your hands. Then pull your hands apart, again and again, to start the disc spinning. It will spin first one way and then the other as the string twists and untwists.

Do this under a neon light and flashes of red and green will appear mysteriously on the disc.

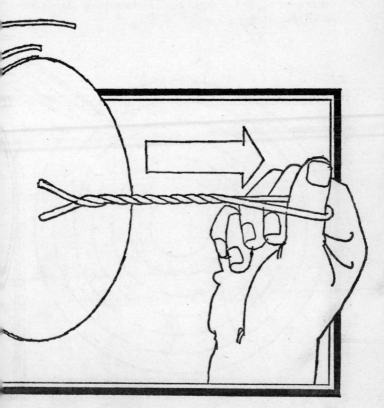

Another colour-creating whizzer

You will need: material described on page 93

Here is a black and white pattern which will turn into complicated wheels of colour when spun around.

1 Prepare a 6 cm disc of white card and draw on it circles of 5.5 cm, 5 cm radius and so on, one inside the other and using the same centre, decreasing the radius of each circle by 5 mm.

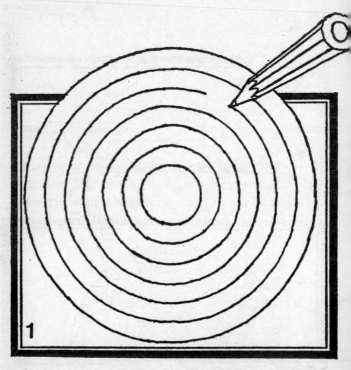

2 Now divide the disc into thirty-two equal segments. Do this by quartering the disc with vertical and horizontal lines through the centre; then draw lines at 45° through the centre to divide it into eighths; then divide each eighth into four equal parts.

3 Cut out a half-circle of black paper of 6 cm radius. Draw half-circles on it like those on the disc; then draw radial lines to divide it into eight equal segments.

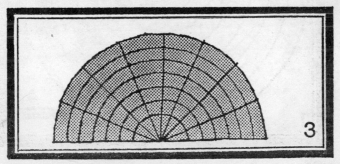

4 Cut pieces from the black paper and stick them to the disc to re-create this pattern. Cut and stick as you go along to avoid getting in a muddle. You will not need every piece of black paper.

Use this disc to make a whizzer as shown on page 96.

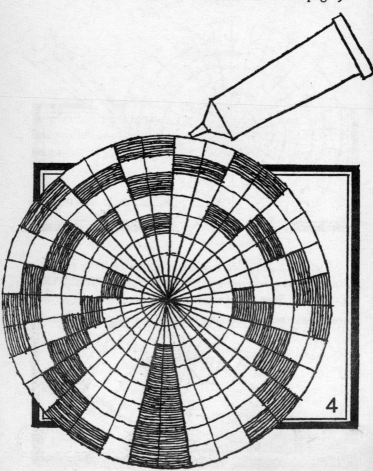

Jacob's ladder

You will need: strip of hard balsa wood, 1 cm thick
length of cotton tape, not more than
1.5 cm wide
pencil
ruler
scissors
craft knife
glue

This is an old folk toy which has been revived in recent years. Once you have prepared the material it is not difficult to put together, provided you follow the steps carefully. Balsa wood can be bought in shops selling kits for model aircraft.

1 Prepare seven pieces of balsa, 6 cm × 10 cm, and eighteen pieces of tape, 15 cm long.

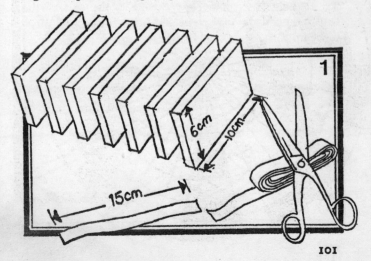

2 Glue three pieces of tape to each of six pieces of balsa like this. That is to say, glue the ends of two pieces of tape (with an overlap of about 1 cm) to the top surface of the balsa at right; and glue one piece similarly to the top surface at centre left.

Study the following drawings carefully to see how the balsa pieces and their tapes should be arranged before assembling.

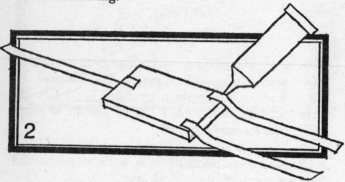

3 Arrange two pieces like this. Lift the end of the centre tape of the first piece and bring the second piece right up to it.

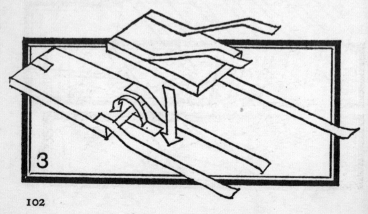

4 Glue the three tape ends to the top surface of the second piece.

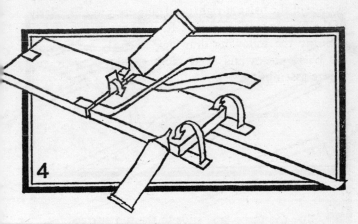

5 Raise the centre tape of the second piece and bring the third piece into position.

6 Glue the three tape ends to the under surface. You will have to turn everything over to do this, but do not forget to return to this position before continuing.

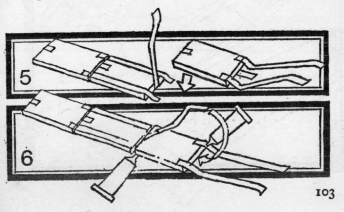

7 Lift the end of the centre tape on the third piece and bring the fourth piece into position.

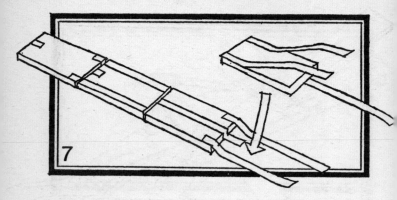

8 Glue the three tape ends to the top surface.

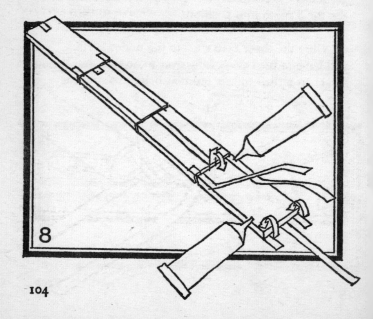

9 Raise the centre tape of the fourth piece and bring the fifth piece into position.

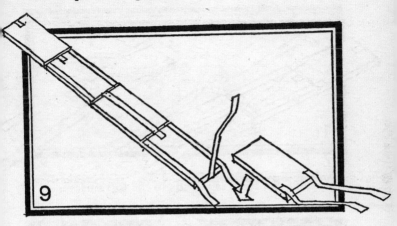

10 Glue the three tape ends to the under surface of the fifth piece. Once again you will have to turn everything over and then return to this position.

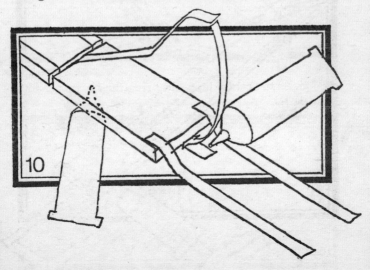

11 Raise the end of the centre tape of the fifth piece and bring the sixth piece into position.

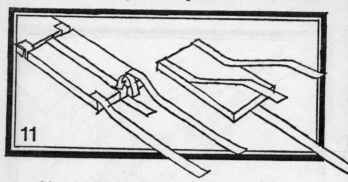

12 Glue the three tape ends to the top surface.

13 Raise the centre tape and bring the final piece into position.

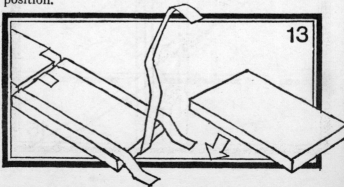

14 Glue the three tape ends to the under surface to complete the Jacob's ladder.

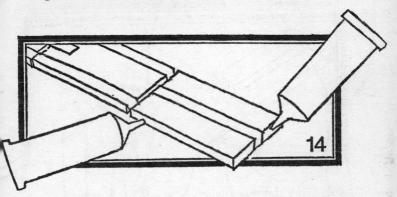

15 Hold the end piece like this and turn your wrist.

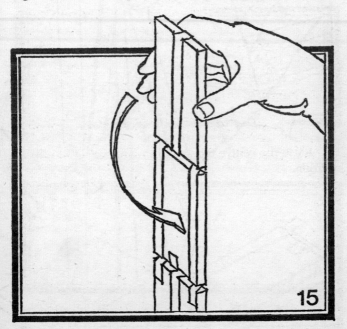

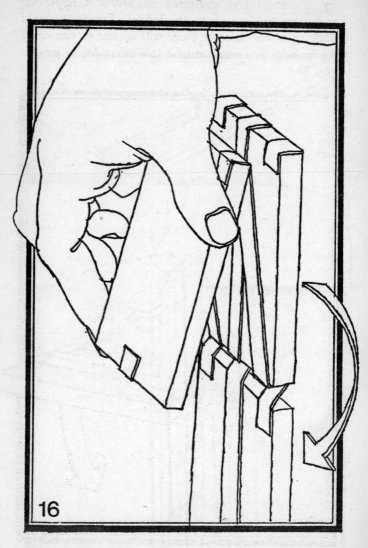

16

17 ... and the second piece will follow it, appearing to run all the way down the ladder. Turn your wrist back again and another piece will appear to run down the ladder. You can continue this effect for as long as you like.

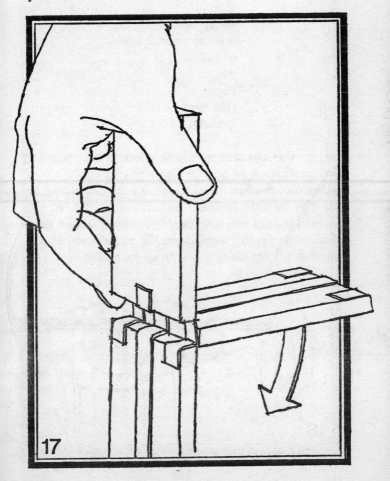

17

Weather prophets

You will need:
  empty cigar box
  cork
  catgut (or a hair from your head)
  glue
  sticky tape
  scissors or craft knife
  pencil
  ruler
  paper
  thin card
  bradawl

Catgut, the mechanism which operates the weather prophets, is not so easy to find nowadays. Old violin strings (not modern ones) were made of catgut and so you may be able to find a broken string from an old violin to use; or you may be able to buy it from a shop which sells angling equipment. If you cannot obtain catgut at all, try using a hair from your head.

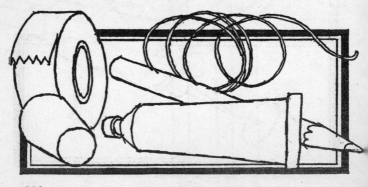

1 Cut the catgut (or hair) so that it is not quite as long as the width of the box.

2 Bore a hole through the centre of the cork.

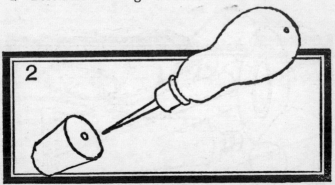

3 Thread one end of the catgut into the cork and fix it with glue.

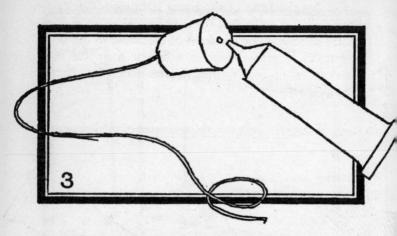

4 Prepare a strip of card about 2 cm wide and about three-quarters as long as the box. Find the exact centre of this strip and make a hole there. Thread the free end of the catgut through it and attach it to the underside with sticky tape.

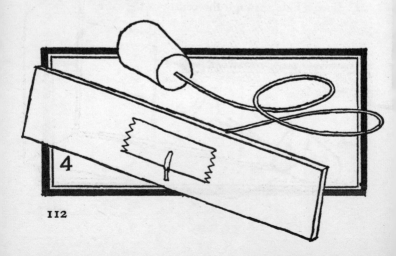

5 Glue the cork to the box at top centre. The strip of card should hang and form a sort of swinging platform.

Cut out the front of the house from card. Cut two large doors or archways; then cut away the base of the centre column. Glue the front of the house to the box and make sure that there is sufficient room for the platform, when it is turned, to pass under the centre column.

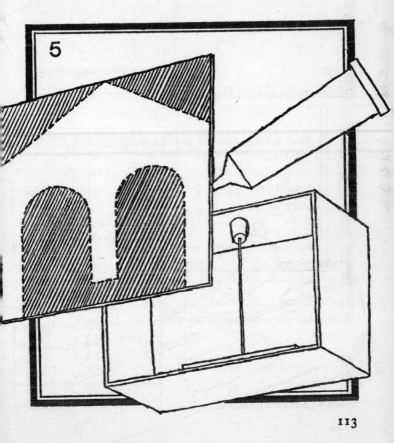

6 To make the weather prophets themselves – the little man and woman who live in the house – prepare two small rectangles of paper, about 3 cm × 6 cm. Place them together and turn up the bottom edges . . .

7 . . . and then fold in half, long edges together.

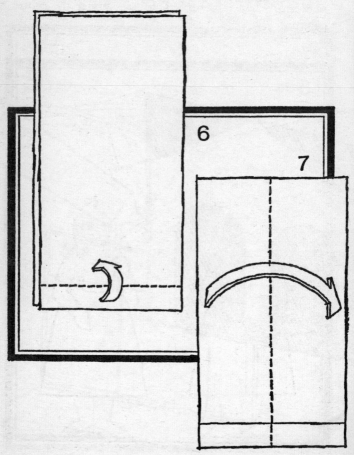

8 With the folded edge at the left, cut an outline like this and throw away the shaded area. Open up and separate the two layers.

9 Turn one piece into a man wearing a raincoat and the other into a woman wearing a summer dress.

10 Now prepare two smaller scraps of paper, about 1.5 cm × 3 cm. Place these together and fold in half. With the folded edge at the left, cut a full, rounded curve. Open up and separate the pieces; throw away the shaded area.

11 This shape can be used to make an umbrella for the man and a flower basket for the woman . . .

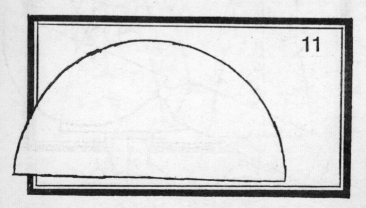

12

13 The man with the umbrella should come out of his house when rain is likely; the woman should come out on fine days. So notice which way the platform tends to turn before fixing your figures to it. When you are sure which ends are the correct ones, glue the man and woman in place, using the tabs behind their feet. Fix labels marked 'Wet' and 'Fine' above the doors and finish by decorating with inks or paints.

Climbing sailor

You will need: sheet of balsa, about 3 mm thick
pencil
ruler
craft knife
glue
six pins
rubber band
scrap of paper
pair of pliers
smooth string (at least 50 cm long)

1 Prepare two rectangles of balsa measuring 2 cm × 5 cm; four rectangles measuring 1.5 cm × 4 cm; and four rectangles measuring 1 cm × 3 cm.

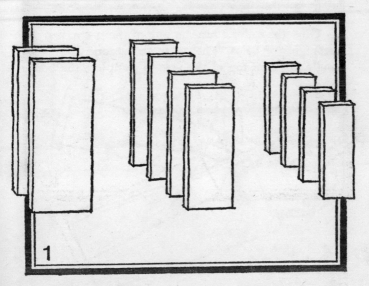

2 On a scrap of paper about 2.5 cm × 4 cm, draw a sailor's head. Leave plenty of space at the bottom of the paper.

3 Now cut around the head.

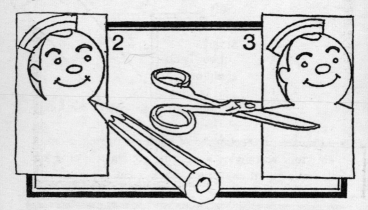

4 Glue the sailor's head to one of the 2 cm × 5 cm rectangles of balsa. Then glue the second large rectangle flush on top of the first to complete the body.

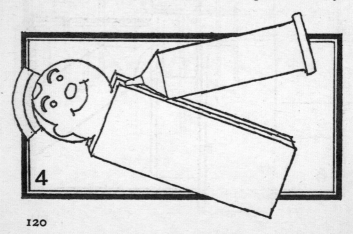

5 Form the 1 cm × 3 cm rectangles into two arms like this . . .

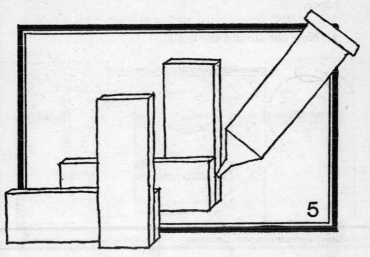

6 . . . and then form the 1.5 cm × 4 cm rectangles into two legs like this.

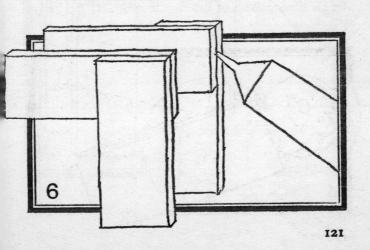

7 Glue the two arms to the body. Attach the legs to the body by pushing a pin through all the layers . . .

8 . . . and bending the end of the pin with a pair of pliers. Nip off the point.

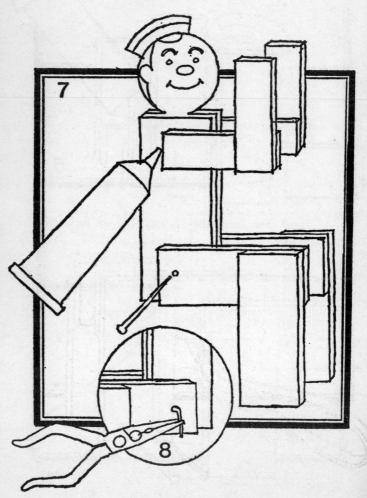

9 Push three more pins into position; one passes through both arms and two pass through the legs. Turn down the pointed ends of the pins and nip off. Place a rubber band between the thighs . . .

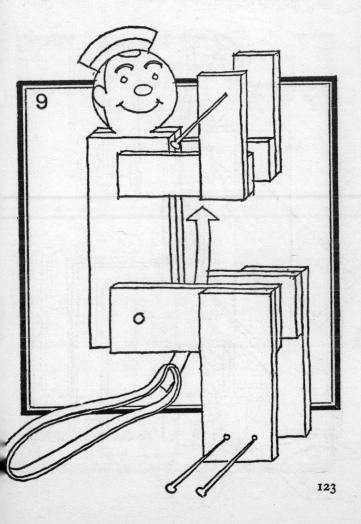

... and pass a pin through both thighs so that the rubber band is looped on to it. Bend and nip off the pointed end of the pin. Bring one end of the piece of string down between the arms and legs of the sailor and up between the two pins at his feet.

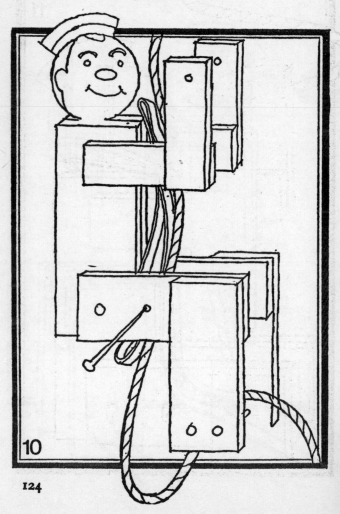

11

Pin the rubber band to the sailor's body behind his neck, after taking up the slack.

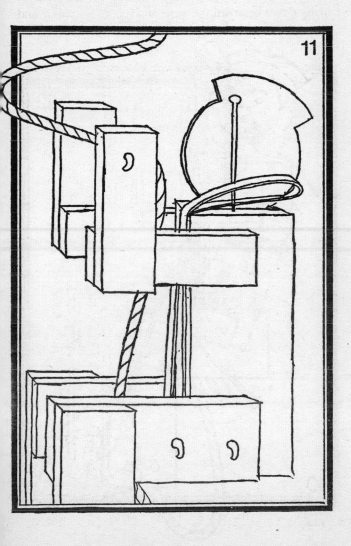

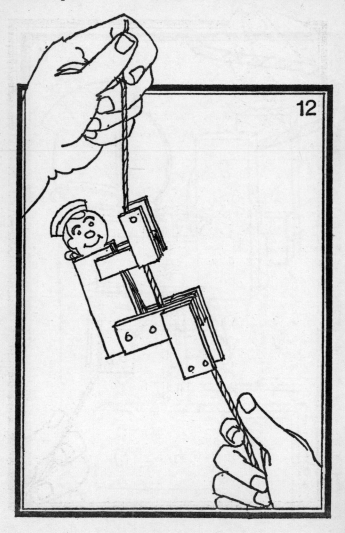

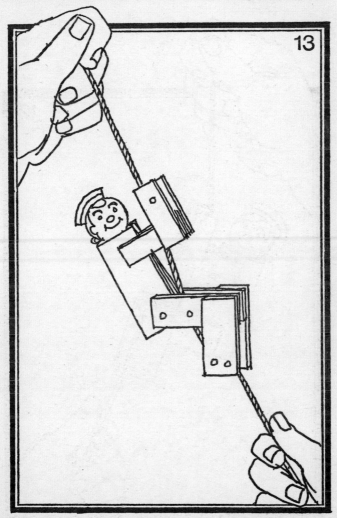

13